Coloring book for kids
Amazing Coloring

- ❖ **Animals**
- ❖ **Fruits**
- ❖ **Vegetables**
- ❖ **Flowers**
- ❖ **Trees**
- ❖ **Foods**

Animals Coloring

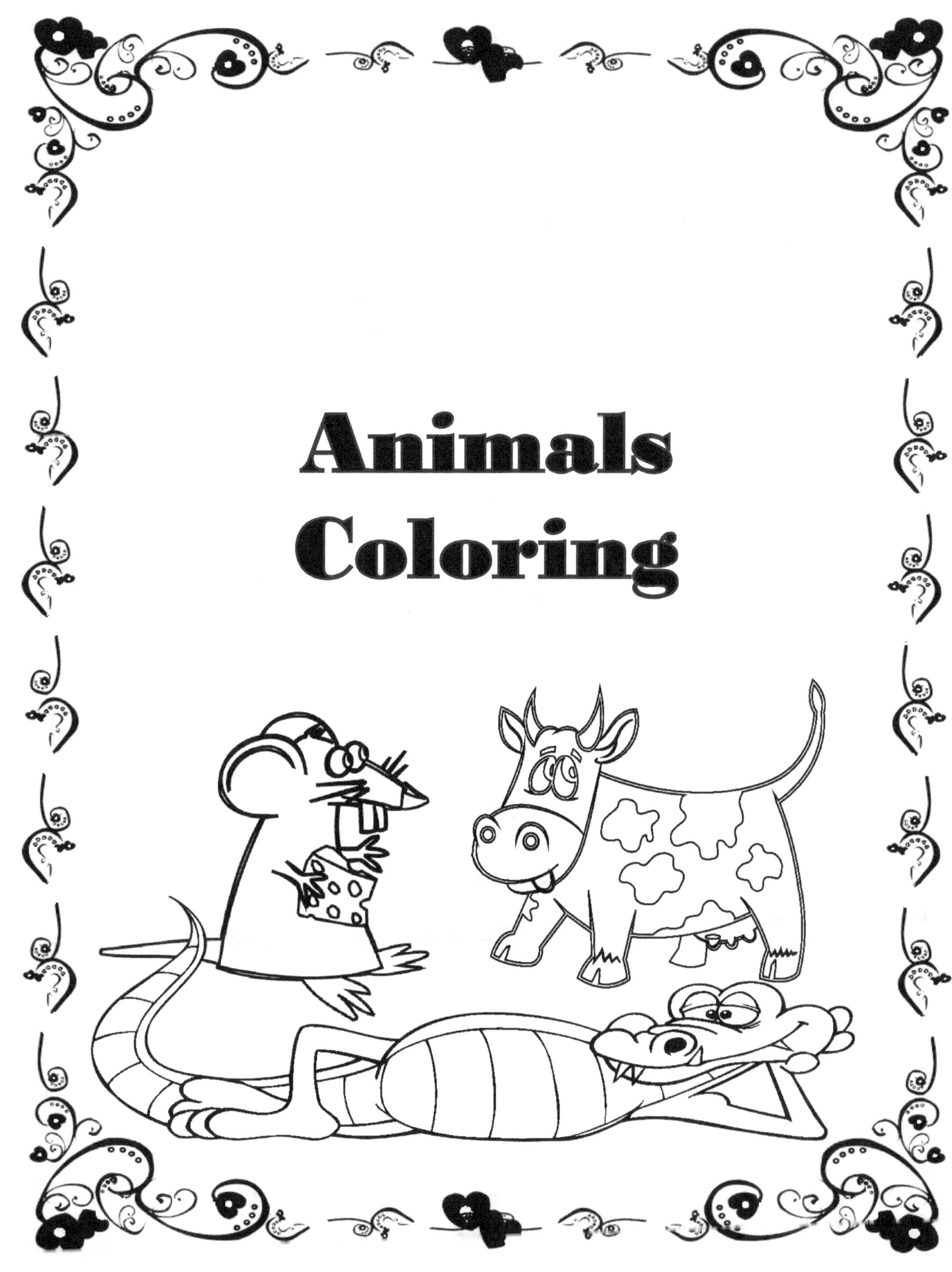

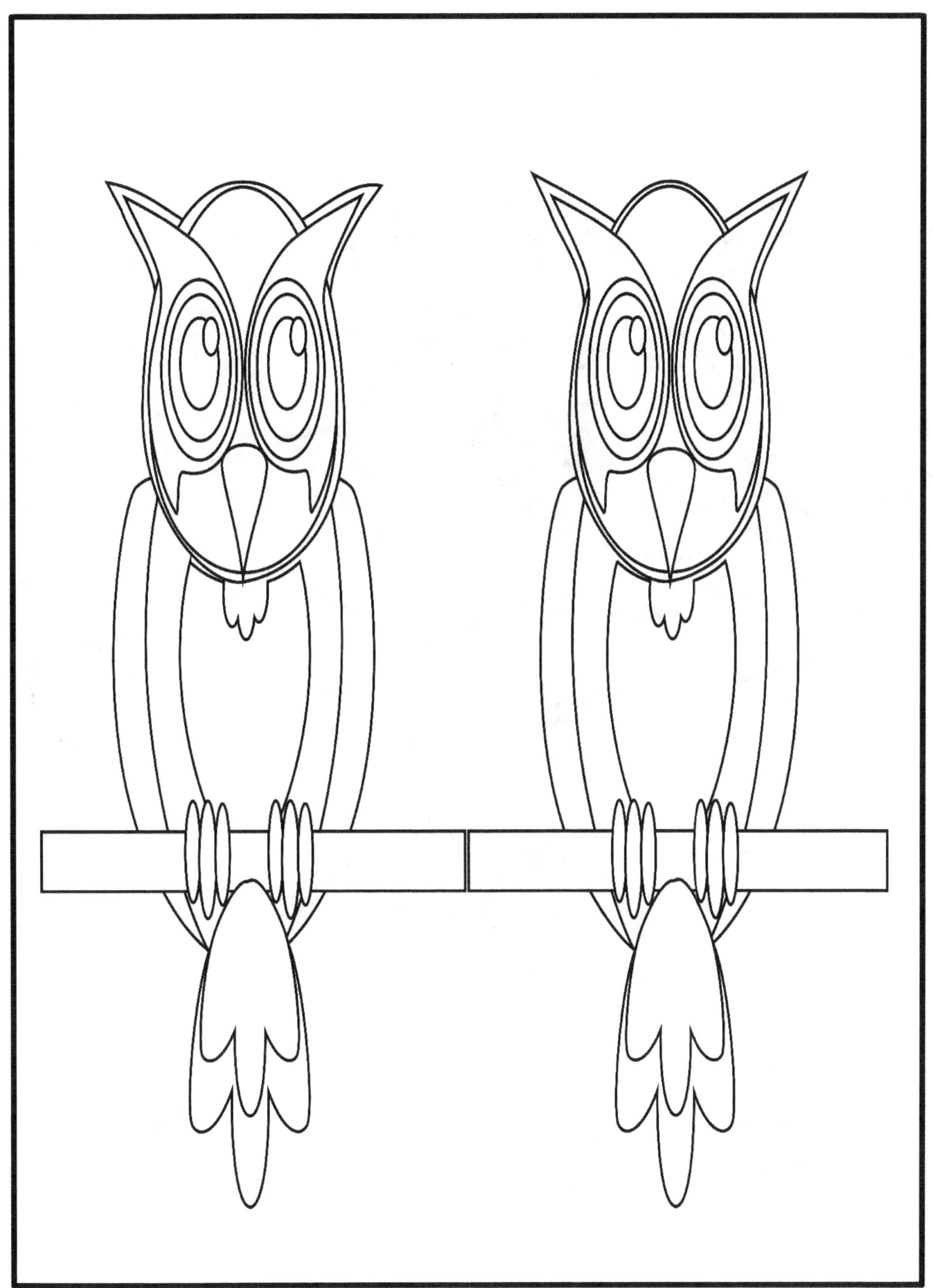

Fruits Coloring

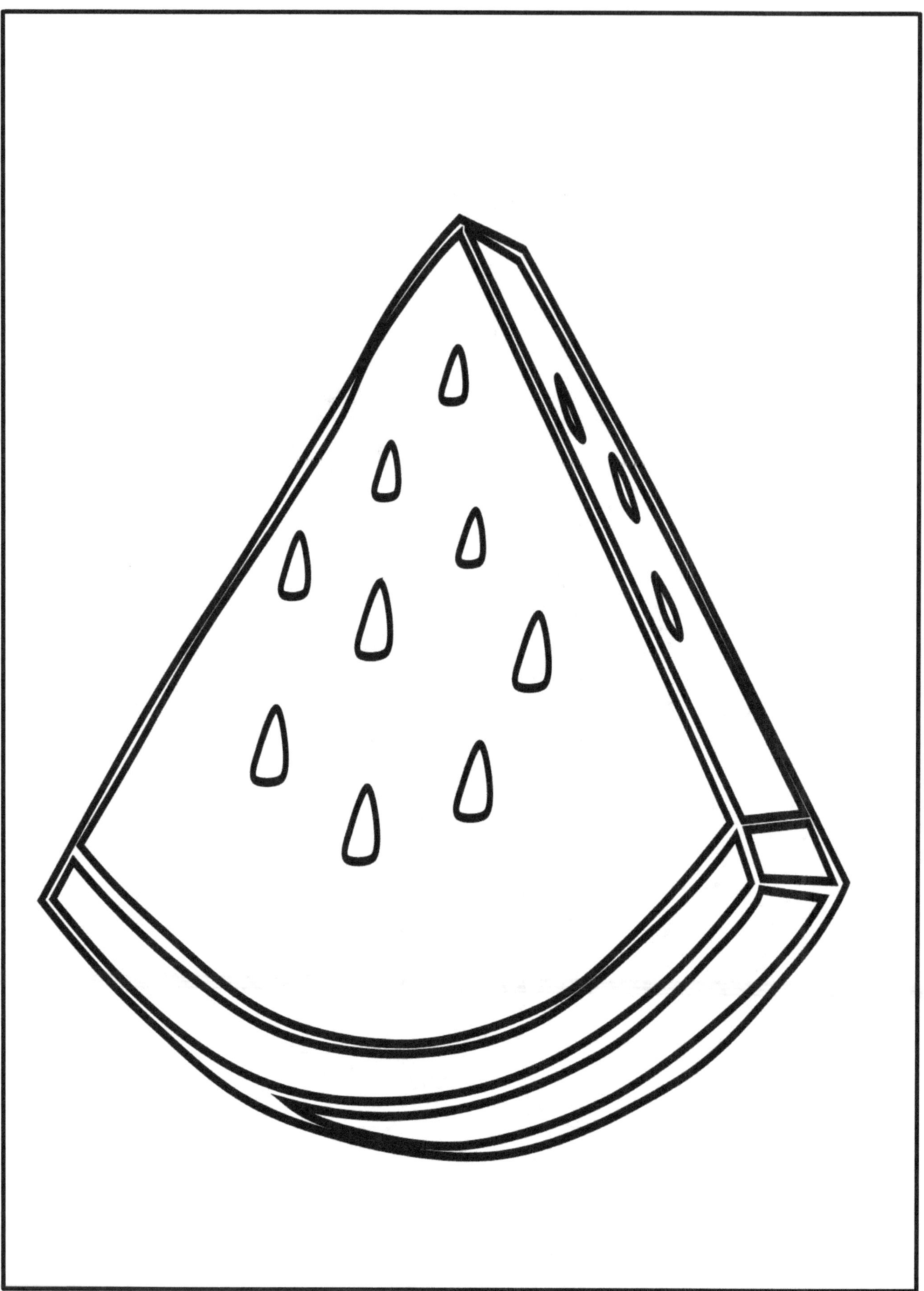

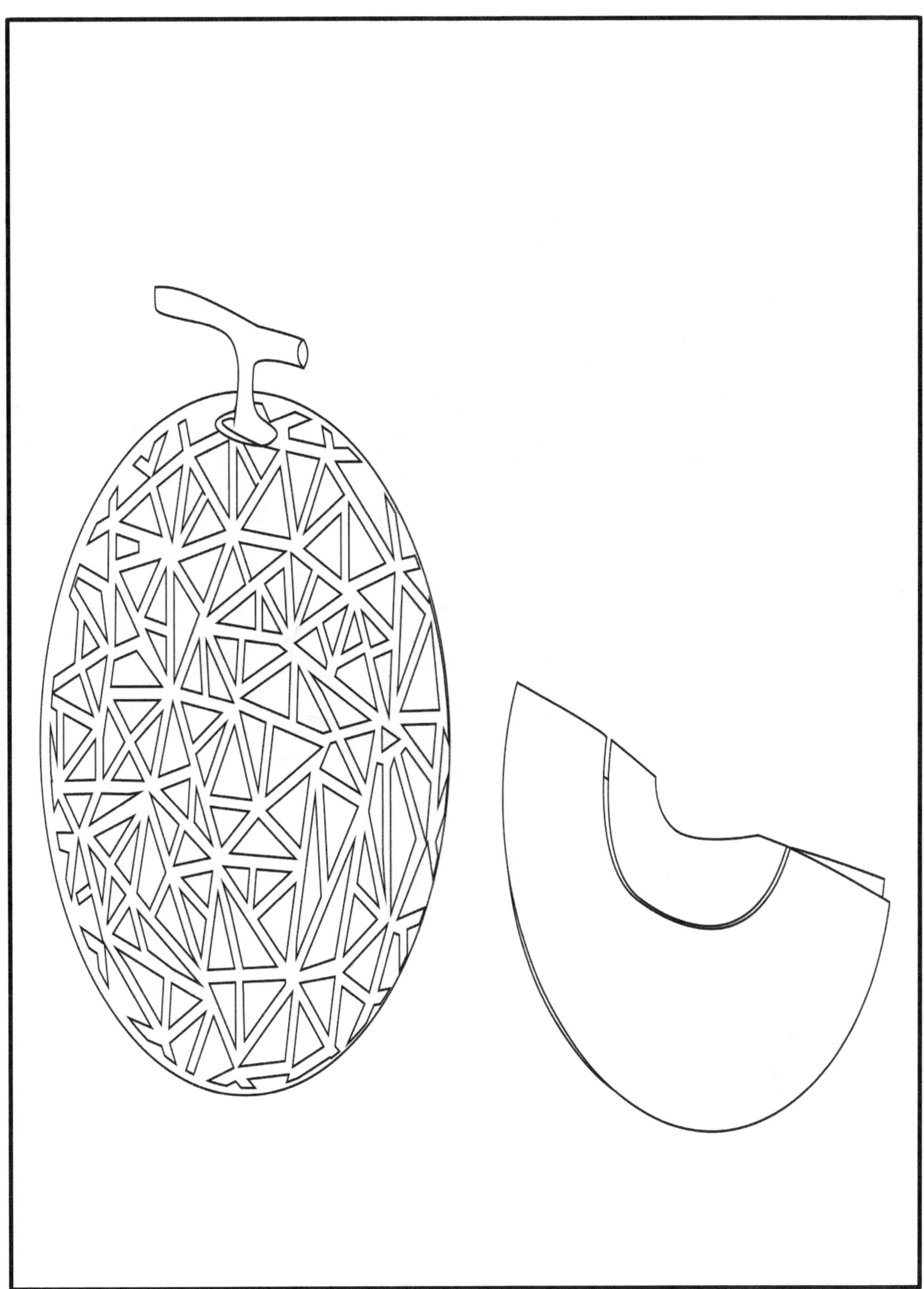

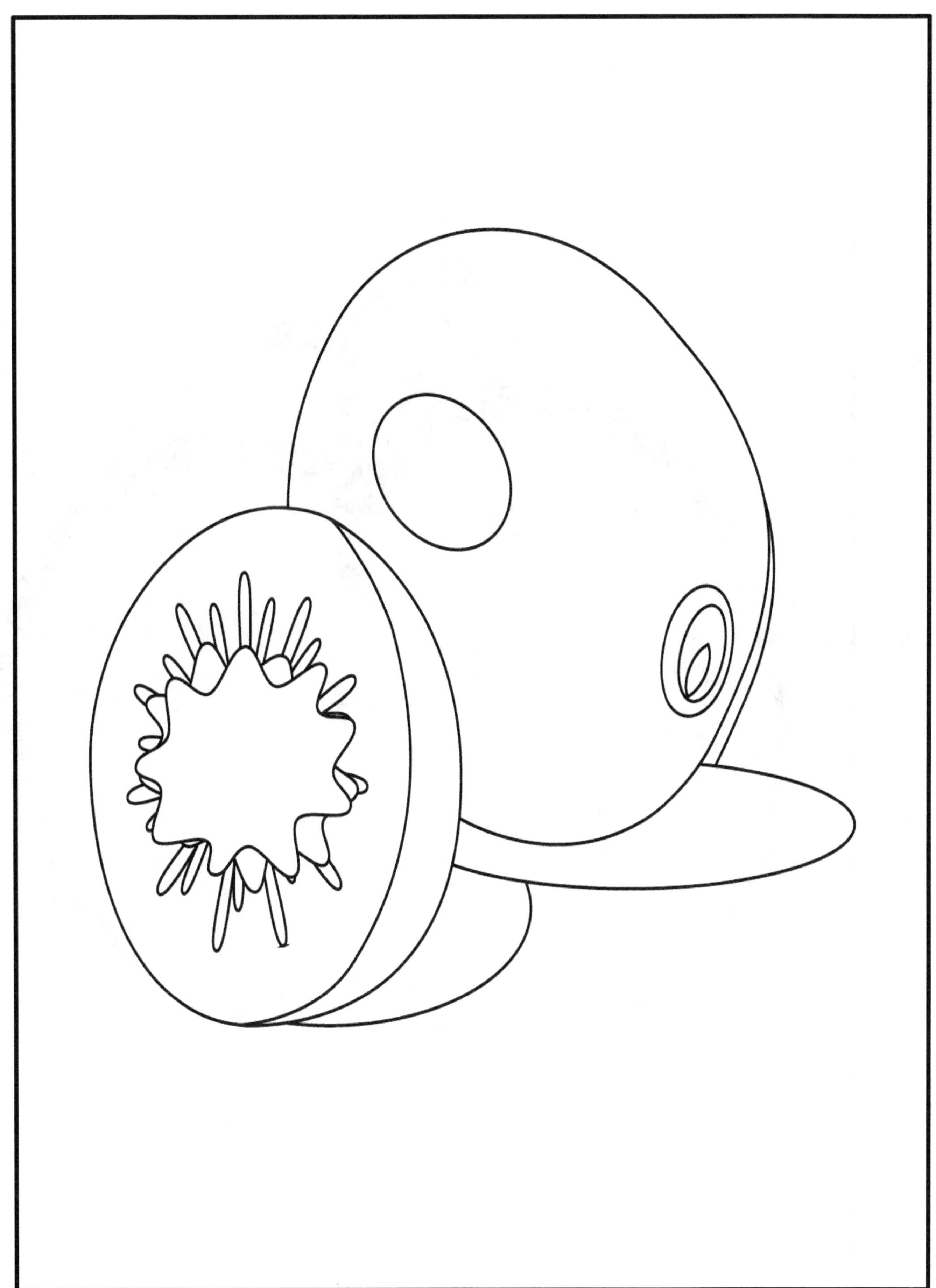

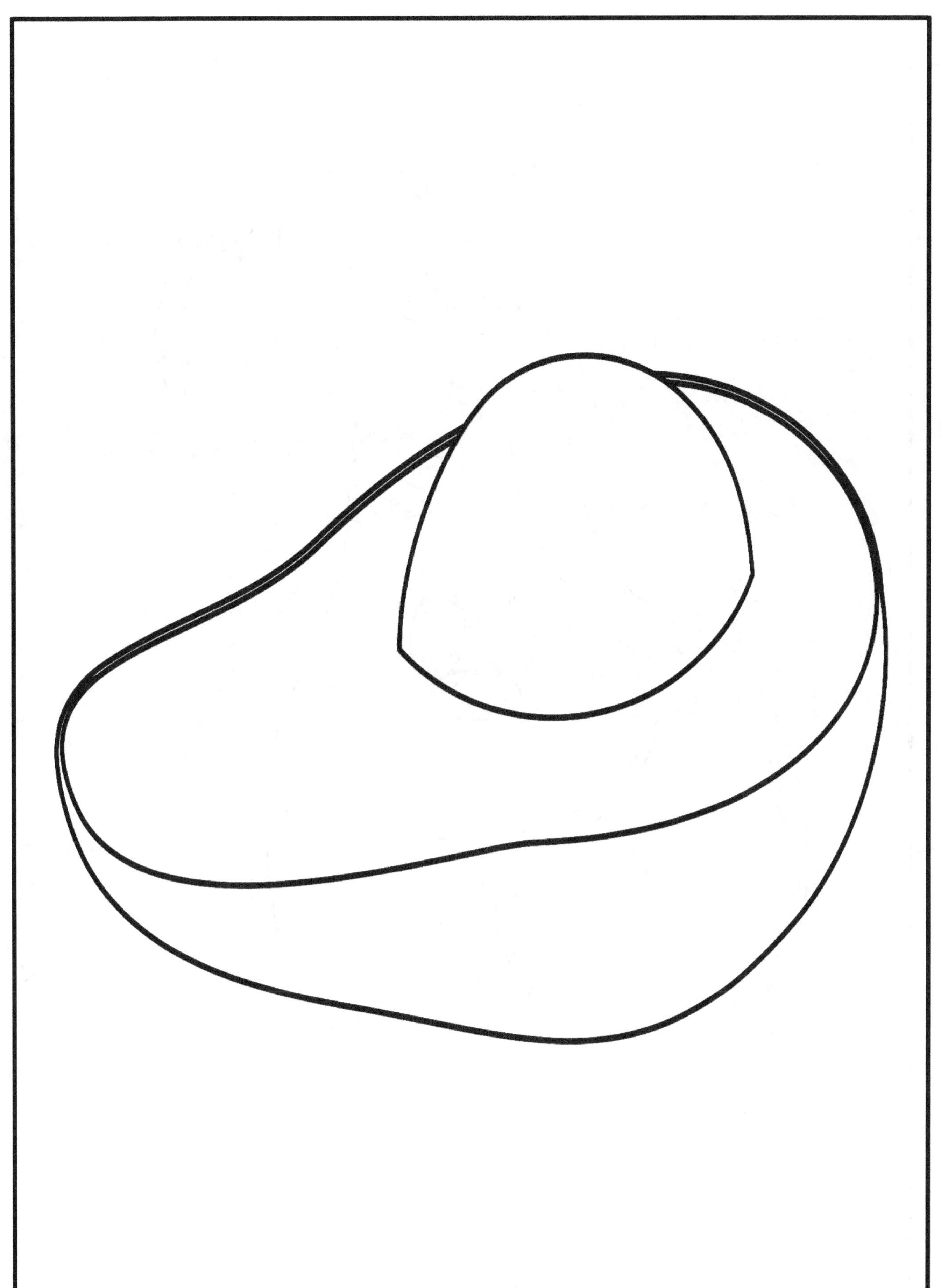

Vegetables Coloring

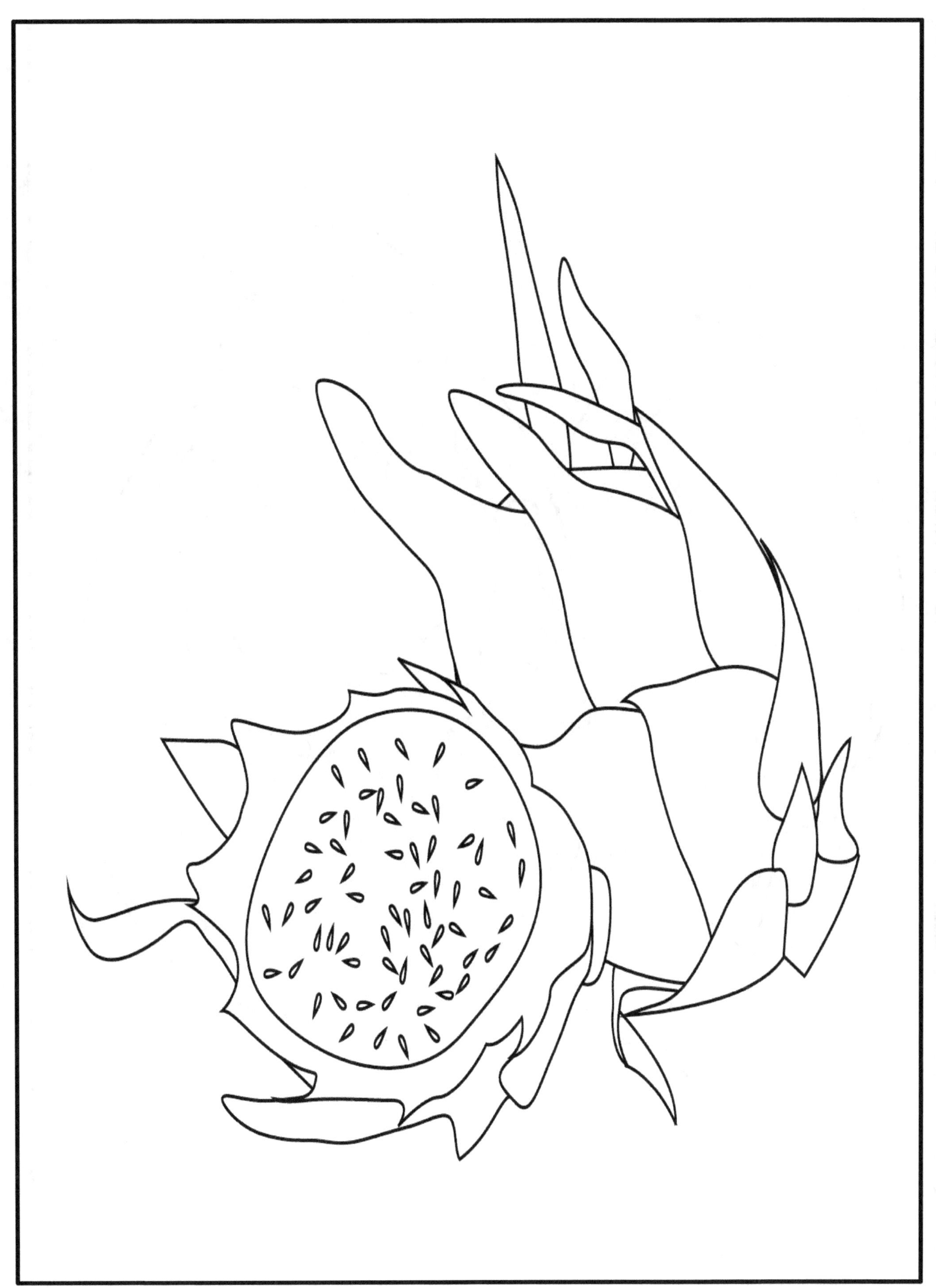

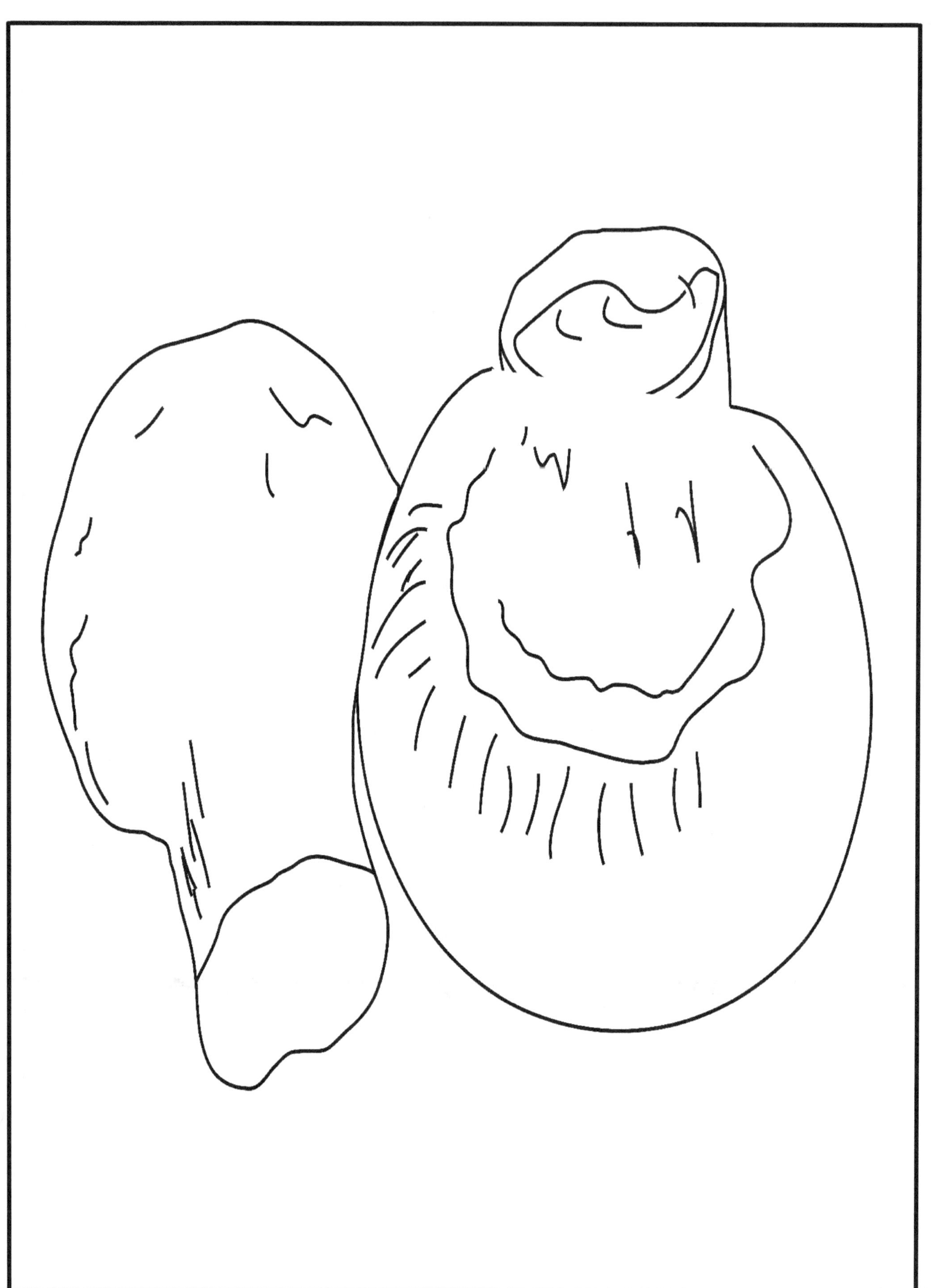

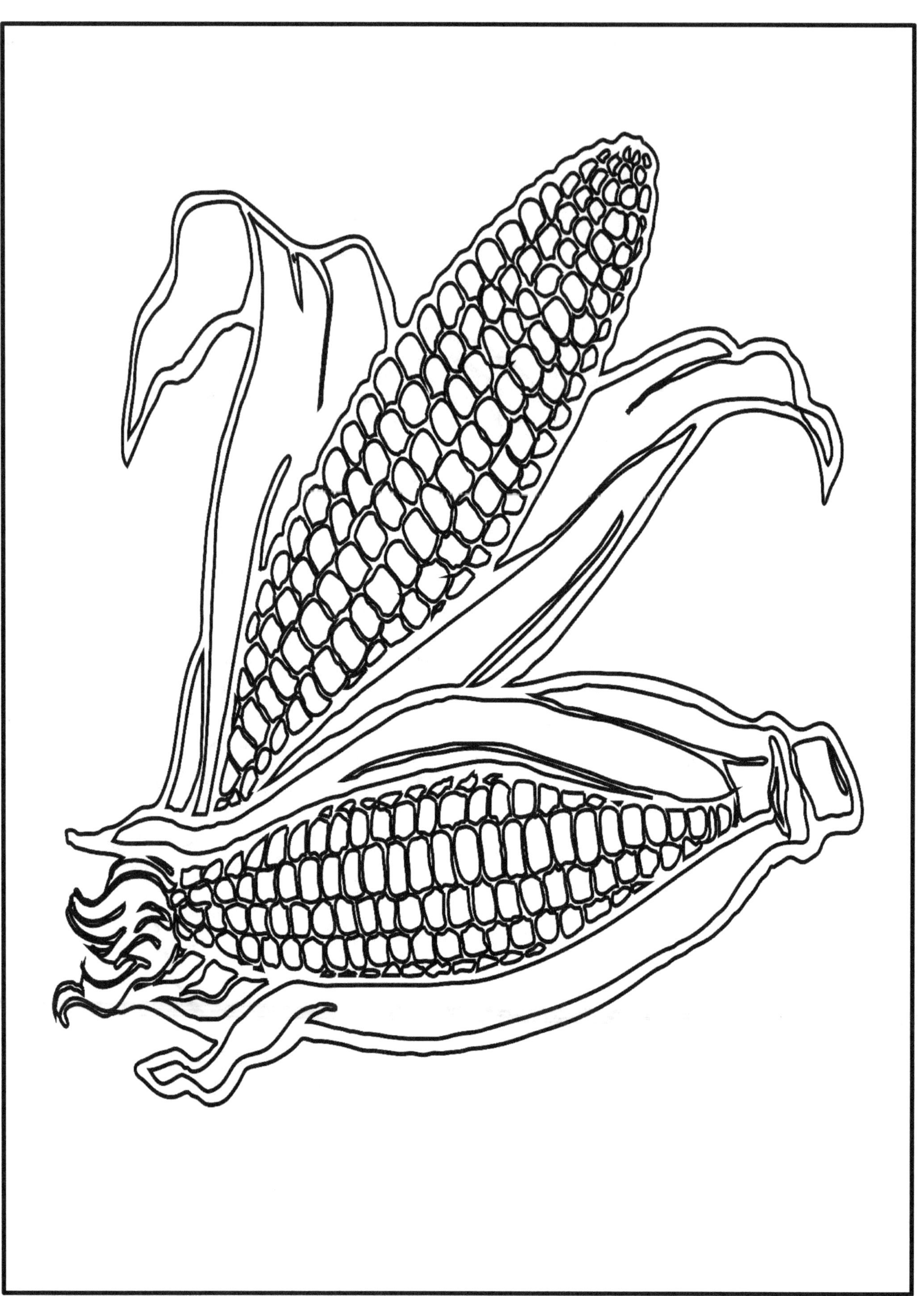

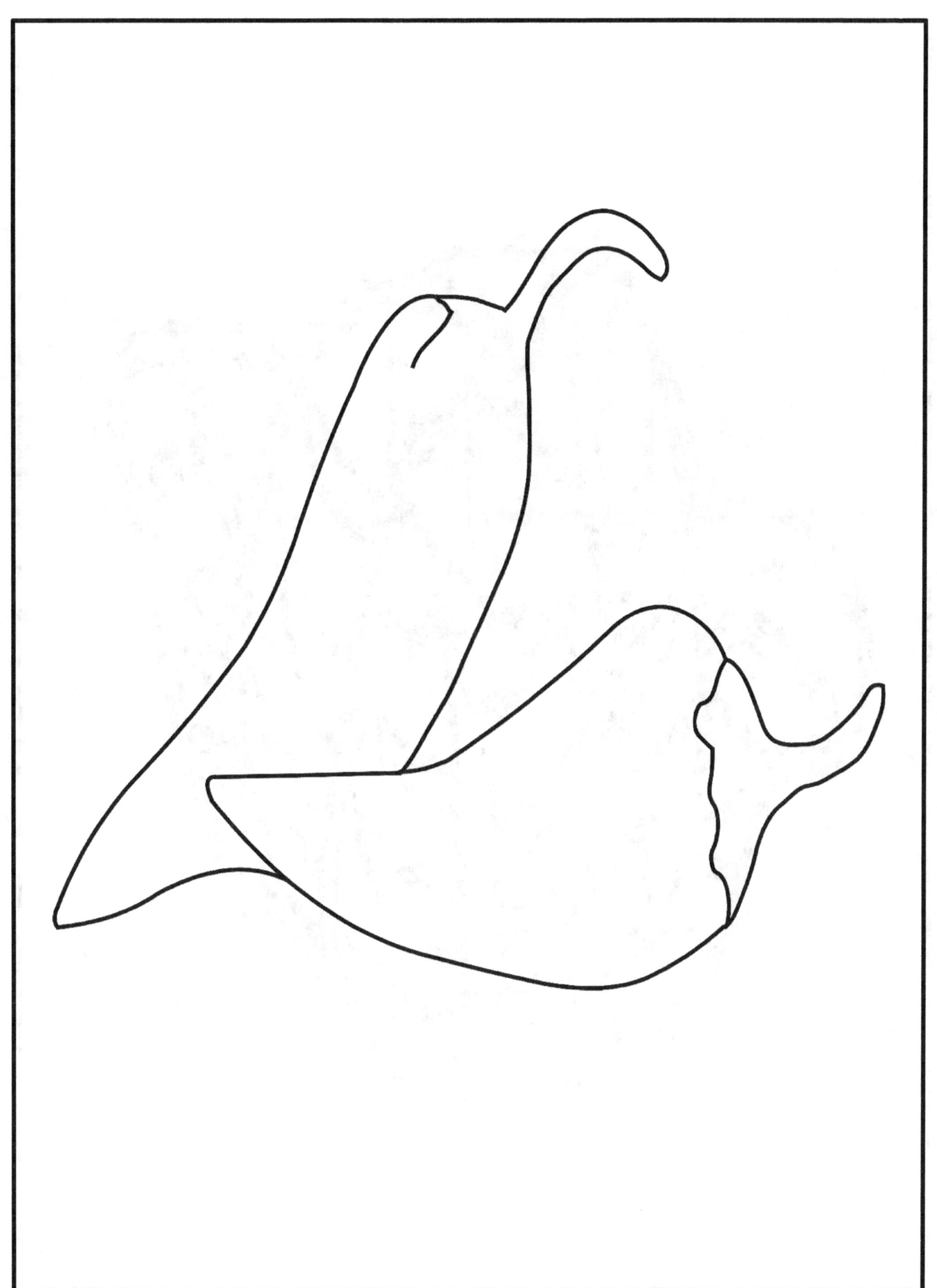

Trees and Flowers Coloring

Foods Coloring

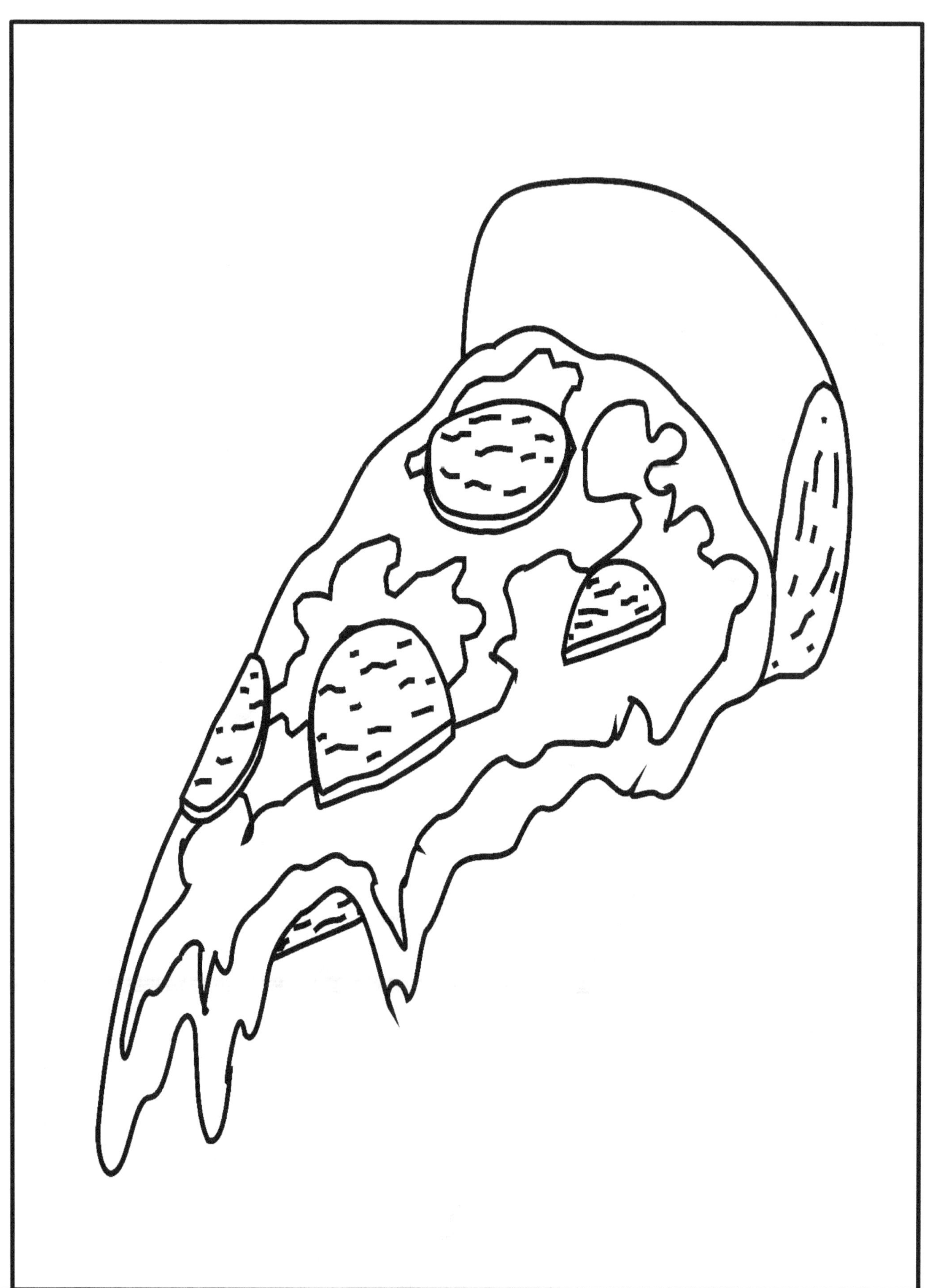

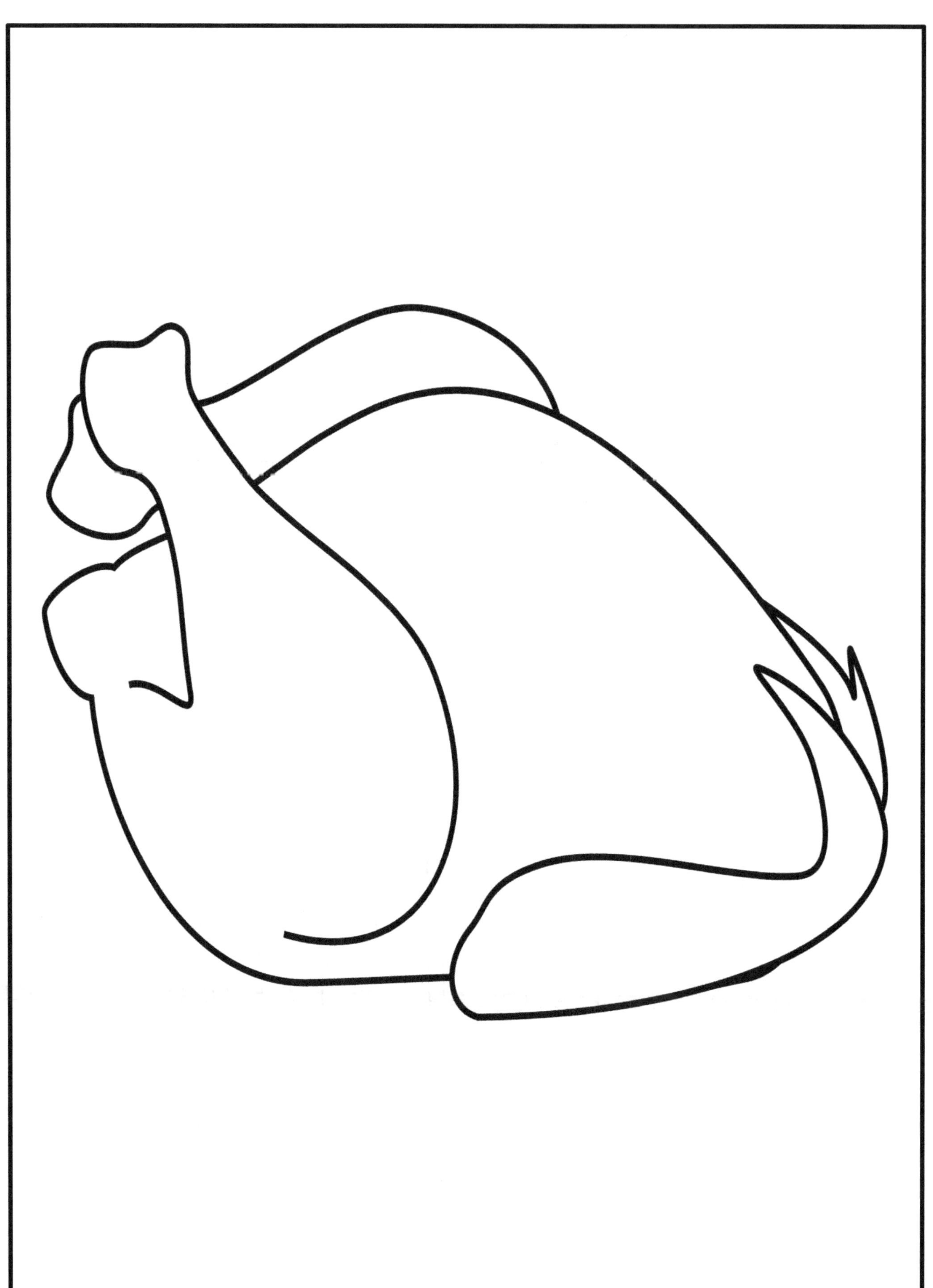

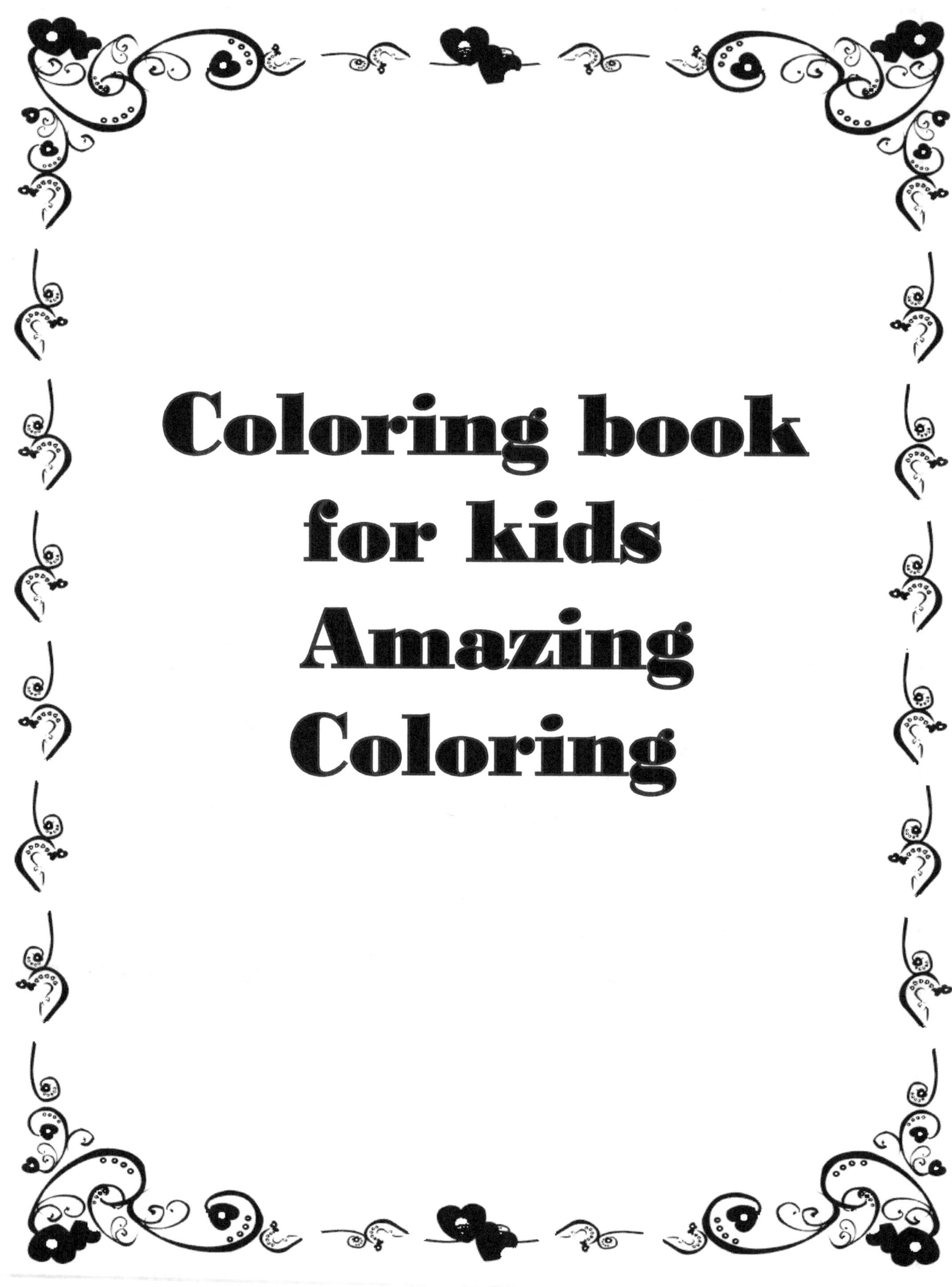

Coloring book for kids Amazing Coloring